D0788030

JR. GRAPHIC AMERICAN INVENTORS

ROBERT FULTON

Steven Roberts

PowerKiDS press

New York

Published in 2013 by The Rosen Publishing Group, Inc.
29 East 21st Street, New York, NY 10010

First Edition

Editor: Joanne Randolph

Book Design: Planman Technologies

Illustrations: Planman Technologies

Library of Congress Cataloging-in-Publication Data

Roberts, Steven.

 Robert Fulton / by Steven Roberts. — 1st ed.

   p. cm. — (Jr. graphic American inventors)

Includes index.

 ISBN 978-1-4777-0077-8 (library binding) — ISBN 978-1-4777-0139-3 (pbk.) — ISBN 978-1-4777-0140-9 (6-pack)

1. Fulton, Robert, 1765-1815—Juvenile literature. 2. Marine engineers—United States—Biography—Juvenile literature. 3. Inventors—United States—Biography—Juvenile literature. 4. Steamboats—Juvenile literature. I. Title.

VM140.F9R63 2013

 623.82'4092—dc23

 [B]

                                        2012020630

Manufactured in the United States of America

CPSIA Compliance Information: Batch #W13PK1: For Further Information contact Rosen Publishing, New York, New York at 1-800-237-9932

Contents

Introduction   3

Main Characters   3

Robert Fulton   4

Timeline   22

Glossary   23

Index and Websites   24

Introduction

Robert Fulton was a man of many talents. He started out as an artist and created the first **panorama** ever shown in Paris. He soon turned to engineering and designed **canals** and bridges. Then he became an inventor and built the first successful submarine, the *Nautilus*. Today he is most famous as the inventor of the first **commercial** steamboat, which made modern sea travel possible.

Main Characters

Napoleon Bonaparte (1769–1821) Military leader who became emperor of France.

Harriet Livingston Fulton (c. 1787–c. 1826) Robert Fulton's wife.

May Smith Fulton (?–?) Robert Fulton's mother.

Robert Fulton (1765–1815) American artist, engineer, and inventor.

Robert Livingston (1746–1813) American ambassador to France and business partner of Fulton.

Charles Stanhope, 3rd Earl Stanhope (1753–1816) British **nobleman** and friend of Robert Fulton.

Benjamin West (1738–1820) American artist living in London. He was the first American artist to gain international recognition for his work.

ROBERT FULTON

SOMEDAY, ROBERT, YOU SHOULD TAKE UP A CRAFT.

ROBERT FULTON WAS BORN NOVEMBER 14, 1765, ON A FARM IN LANCASTER COUNTY, PENNSYLVANIA. LANCASTER, WHERE HE GREW UP, WAS KNOWN AS A CENTER FOR **CRAFTSMEN**.

ROBERT'S FATHER WORKED AS A FARMER, A TAILOR, AND AT OTHER JOBS. WHEN ROBERT WAS EIGHT, HIS FATHER DIED WITHOUT LEAVING A **WILL** OR ANY MONEY.

IT WILL BE HARD TO GET BY, BUT WE'LL MAKE IT.

PREPARE TO FIRE!

WHEN ROBERT WAS NINE, THE AMERICAN REVOLUTION, A WAR IN WHICH AMERICAN COLONISTS FOUGHT FOR INDEPENDENCE FROM BRITAIN, BEGAN. IT LASTED FOR SEVERAL YEARS.

BY THE AGE OF 10, ROBERT SHOWED TALENT AS AN ARTIST. HE FOUND WORK DRAWING DESIGNS FOR LOCAL GUNSMITHS.

NICE WORK. YOU SHOULD BE AN ARTIST.

ROBERT ALSO SHOWED TALENT AS AN ENGINEER. WHEN HE WAS 13 YEARS OLD, HE MADE TOY BOATS **PROPELLED** BY PADDLE WHEELS.

5

ROBERT DECIDED TO BECOME AN ARTIST. AT THE AGE OF 17, HE MOVED TO PHILADELPHIA, WHERE HE FOUND WORK IN A JEWELRY SHOP, PAINTING MINIATURE **PORTRAITS** FOR **LOCKETS** AND RINGS. HE ALSO BEGAN PAINTING LARGER PORTRAITS OF PEOPLE AND LANDSCAPES.

BY 1785, HE HAD MADE ENOUGH MONEY TO BUY HIS MOTHER, MAY, A FARM IN HOPEWELL, PENNSYLVANIA.

ALL THIS IS YOURS NOW, MOTHER.

IT'S WONDERFUL!

ONE OF THE PEOPLE FULTON MET IN PHILADELPHIA WAS BENJAMIN FRANKLIN, WHOSE PORTRAIT HE PAINTED.

MR. FRANKLIN, WOULD YOU SHOW ME SOME OF YOUR INVENTIONS LATER?

I'D LOVE TO, MY BOY.

FRANKLIN AND OTHER **PROMINENT** MEMBERS OF PHILADELPHIA SOCIETY ADVISED FULTON TO GO TO EUROPE TO STUDY PAINTING. IN 1786, FULTON MOVED TO LONDON, ENGLAND.

HOW DO YOU LIKE OUR SHIP, MR. FULTON?

I'VE ALWAYS BEEN INTERESTED IN SHIP CONSTRUCTION. DO YOU MIND IF I LOOK AROUND?

I HAVE BROUGHT LETTERS OF INTRODUCTION FROM FRIENDS IN AMERICA.

I'VE HEARD YOU ARE A VERY TALENTED MAN, MR. FULTON. I THINK YOU WILL DO WELL IN LONDON.

FULTON MET WITH THE ARTIST BENJAMIN WEST AND THEN LIVED WITH HIS FAMILY FOR THE NEXT FEW YEARS. HE STUDIED PAINTING UNDER HIM.

THROUGH WEST, FULTON MET MEMBERS OF THE BRITISH NOBILITY, INCLUDING CHARLES STANHOPE, 3RD EARL STANHOPE, FOR WHOM HE PAINTED PORTRAITS AND LANDSCAPES.

I MUST INTRODUCE YOU TO MY FRIEND, LORD SHELBURNE.

STANHOPE SHARED A COMMON INTEREST WITH FULTON IN THE WAY CANALS, BRIDGES, AND BOATS WERE BUILT. FULTON SHOWED STANHOPE HIS DESIGN FOR A STEAMBOAT.

IT WOULD BE POWERED BY STEAM AND PROPELLED BY PADDLE WHEELS.

ROBERT, YOU SHOULD BE AN ENGINEER!

IN 1793, FULTON GAVE UP PAINTING TO STUDY **CIVIL ENGINEERING**. IN 1794, HE INVENTED A SPECIAL DEVICE FOR RAISING AND LOWERING BOATS IN A CANAL AND A **DREDGING** MACHINE.

IN 1796, FULTON PUBLISHED A *TREATISE ON THE IMPROVEMENT OF CANAL NAVIGATION.* IT PROPOSED A PLAN FOR A COMPLETE SYSTEM OF CANALS RUNNING THROUGHOUT THE BRITISH COUNTRYSIDE.

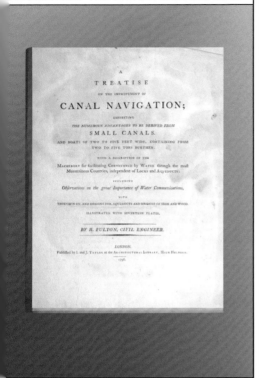

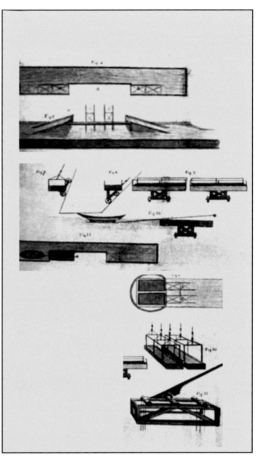

THE BRITISH GOVERNMENT, HOWEVER, WAS NOT INTERESTED IN FULTON'S PLAN. IN 1797, FULTON DECIDED TO LEAVE ENGLAND AND MOVE TO PARIS, FRANCE.

PERHAPS THEY WILL BE MORE INTERESTED IN MY DESIGNS IN FRANCE.

I HAVE SEVERAL FRIENDS THERE YOU CAN CONTACT. I TOLD THEM YOU WERE COMING.

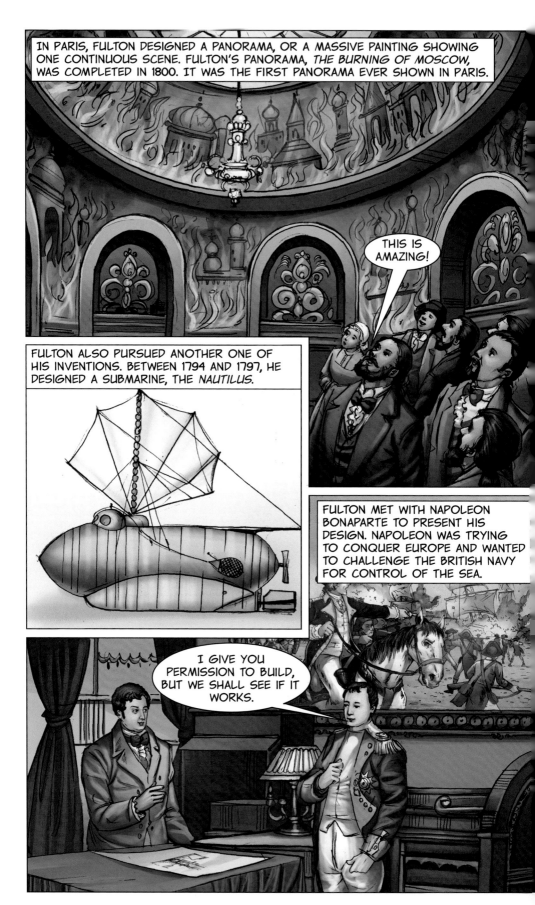

IN PARIS, FULTON DESIGNED A PANORAMA, OR A MASSIVE PAINTING SHOWING ONE CONTINUOUS SCENE. FULTON'S PANORAMA, *THE BURNING OF MOSCOW*, WAS COMPLETED IN 1800. IT WAS THE FIRST PANORAMA EVER SHOWN IN PARIS.

THIS IS AMAZING!

FULTON ALSO PURSUED ANOTHER ONE OF HIS INVENTIONS. BETWEEN 1794 AND 1797, HE DESIGNED A SUBMARINE, THE *NAUTILUS*.

FULTON MET WITH NAPOLEON BONAPARTE TO PRESENT HIS DESIGN. NAPOLEON WAS TRYING TO CONQUER EUROPE AND WANTED TO CHALLENGE THE BRITISH NAVY FOR CONTROL OF THE SEA.

I GIVE YOU PERMISSION TO BUILD, BUT WE SHALL SEE IF IT WORKS.

THE *NAUTILUS* WAS FIRST TESTED ON JULY 29, 1800. IT TOOK 17 MINUTES TO GO 25 FEET (8 M) UNDER WATER. IT WAS THE FIRST SUCCESSFUL SUBMARINE IN HISTORY, AND THE BASICS OF THE DESIGN ARE STILL USED IN SUBMARINES TODAY.

THE *NAUTILUS* HAD AN OBSERVATION DOME ON TOP AND WAS LIT INSIDE BY TWO CANDLES. TWO MEN CRANKING A **PROPELLER** MOVED THE SUBMARINE FORWARD, AND TWO FINS ON THE SIDE MOVED IT UP AND DOWN.

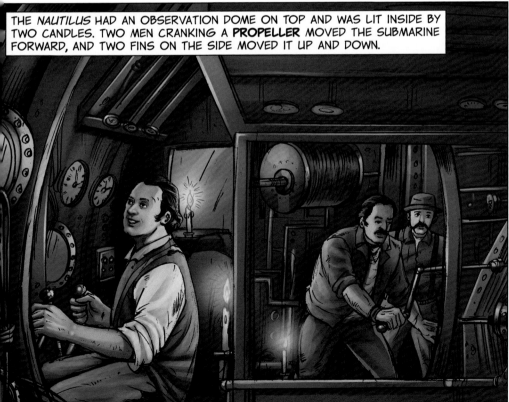

THE *NAUTILUS* ALSO INCLUDED ANOTHER INVENTION, THE **TORPEDO**. THE TORPEDO COULD BE ATTACHED TO THE **HULL** OF A SHIP USING A SPIKE ON THE TOP OF THE SUBMARINE. THE TORPEDO WOULD DETACH FROM THE SUBMARINE. THE SUBMARINE WOULD THEN SPEED AWAY AND **DETONATE** THE TORPEDO USING A LONG LINE.

THE TEST, HOWEVER, WAS NOT A COMPLETE SUCCESS. THE SUBMARINE LEAKED, AND THE TORPEDO FAILED TO SINK THE SHIP USED IN THE TEST. NAPOLEON LOST INTEREST IN FULTON'S INVENTIONS.

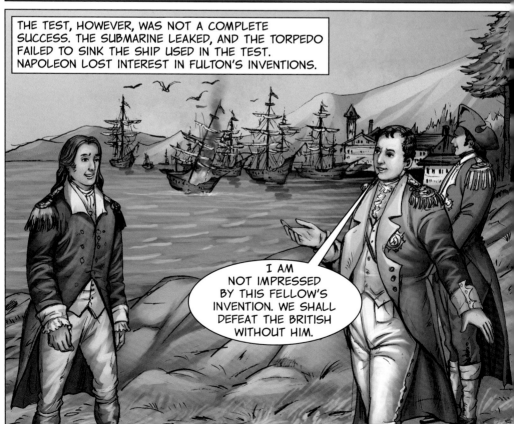

I AM NOT IMPRESSED BY THIS FELLOW'S INVENTION. WE SHALL DEFEAT THE BRITISH WITHOUT HIM.

IT'S A PLEASURE TO MEET A FELLOW AMERICAN IN PARIS.

IN 1801, FULTON'S **FORTUNES** TURNED. HE BECAME FRIENDS WITH ROBERT LIVINGSTON, THE AMERICAN AMBASSADOR TO FRANCE.

LIVINGSTON SHARED FULTON'S INTEREST IN STEAMSHIPS. THEY DECIDED TO BUILD ONE TOGETHER WITH THEIR OWN MONEY USING FULTON'S DESIGN.

WITH YOUR DESIGN AND MY CONNECTIONS IN NEW YORK, WE CAN START OUR OWN BUSINESS.

THIS NEW STEAMSHIP WAS SIMILAR TO A DESIGN CREATED BY JOHN FITCH BUT WITH A MAJOR DIFFERENCE. FITCH'S DESIGN USED PADDLES SHAPED LIKE A DUCK'S WEBBED FOOT, WHICH DID NOT WORK WELL. FULTON'S DESIGN USED A PADDLE WHEEL.

FULTON'S STEAMSHIP DESIGN

FULTON HAD A STEAMSHIP BUILT THAT WAS 66 FEET (20 M) LONG, 8 FEET (2 M) WIDE, AND USED AN EIGHT-HORSEPOWER FRENCH STEAM ENGINE. THE ENGINE, HOWEVER, BROKE THROUGH THE HULL AND THE SHIP SANK.

THE ENGINE WAS TOO HEAVY FOR THE HULL.

NO REASON TO GIVE UP. WE'LL BUILD A BETTER ONE.

FULTON CAME UP WITH NEW DESIGNS, CONDUCTED EXPERIMENTS WITH DIFFERENT HULL SHAPES, AND BUILT MODELS.

FULTON BUILT A NEW STEAMSHIP WITH A STRONGER HULL. THE SECOND TEST WAS A SUCCESS.

NOW WE NEED TO BUILD A MUCH BIGGER SHIP.

WE SHOULD RETURN TO AMERICA TO MAKE IT AS SOON AS POSSIBLE.

FULTON WANTED A MORE POWERFUL ENGINE. HE WROTE TO BOULTON AND WATT, A COMPANY THAT MADE THE BEST STEAM ENGINES IN THE WORLD, IN ENGLAND, AND ORDERED A MASSIVE SPECIALLY-MADE 24-HORSEPOWER ENGINE.

WHAT DOES THIS MAN FULTON WANT THE ENGINE FOR?

HE DIDN'T SAY. I THINK HE'S CRAZY.

IN 1804, FULTON RETURNED TO LONDON. HE PLANNED ON TRANSPORTING THE BOULTON AND WATT ENGINE TO NEW YORK, WHERE HE WOULD CONTINUE HIS WORK ON A STEAMSHIP.

SO WHAT DO YOU THINK OF OUR SHIP, MR. FULTON?

I THINK YOU SHOULD REPLACE THESE SAILS WITH A STEAM ENGINE.

I NEED THIS ENGINE TO CONTINUE MY WORK!

I'M SORRY. WE CAN'T RISK HAVING ONE OF OUR ENGINES FALL INTO THE HANDS OF THE FRENCH.

BY THEN, BRITAIN WAS AT WAR WITH FRANCE AND WOULD NOT ALLOW STEAM ENGINES TO BE **SHIPPED** OUT OF THE COUNTRY. FULTON WOULD HAVE TO WAIT.

WE ARE VERY INTERESTED IN YOUR DESIGN FOR THIS THING CALLED A TORPEDO. IT MIGHT HELP US BEAT THE FRENCH.

THE BRITISH NAVY, HOWEVER, WAS INTERESTED IN FULTON'S DESIGNS FOR A SUBMARINE AND TORPEDO. THE NAVY HIRED HIM TO CONTINUE WORKING ON THEM.

HE DESIGNED A NEW AND IMPROVED TORPEDO. IN OCTOBER 1805, THE BRITISH NAVY PROVIDED A SHIP TO TEST IT. FULTON'S TORPEDO BLEW THE SHIP IN HALF.

EXCELLENT!

THAT SAME MONTH, THE BRITISH NAVY DEFEATED THE FRENCH NAVY IN THE BATTLE OF TRAFALGAR. THE BRITISH NOW CONTROLLED THE SEAS AND DECIDED THEY NO LONGER NEEDED FULTON'S SUBMARINE OR TORPEDO.

THE BRITISH FINALLY GAVE FULTON PERMISSION TO TAKE HIS ENGINE TO AMERICA. HE SET SAIL AND ARRIVED IN NEW YORK IN DECEMBER 1806.

WELCOME TO AMERICA, SIR.

IT'S GOOD TO BE HOME.

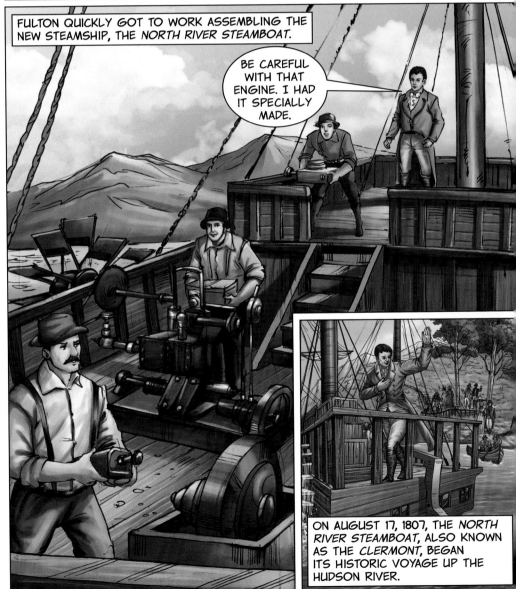

FULTON QUICKLY GOT TO WORK ASSEMBLING THE NEW STEAMSHIP, THE *NORTH RIVER STEAMBOAT*.

BE CAREFUL WITH THAT ENGINE. I HAD IT SPECIALLY MADE.

ON AUGUST 17, 1807, THE *NORTH RIVER STEAMBOAT*, ALSO KNOWN AS THE *CLERMONT*, BEGAN ITS HISTORIC VOYAGE UP THE HUDSON RIVER.

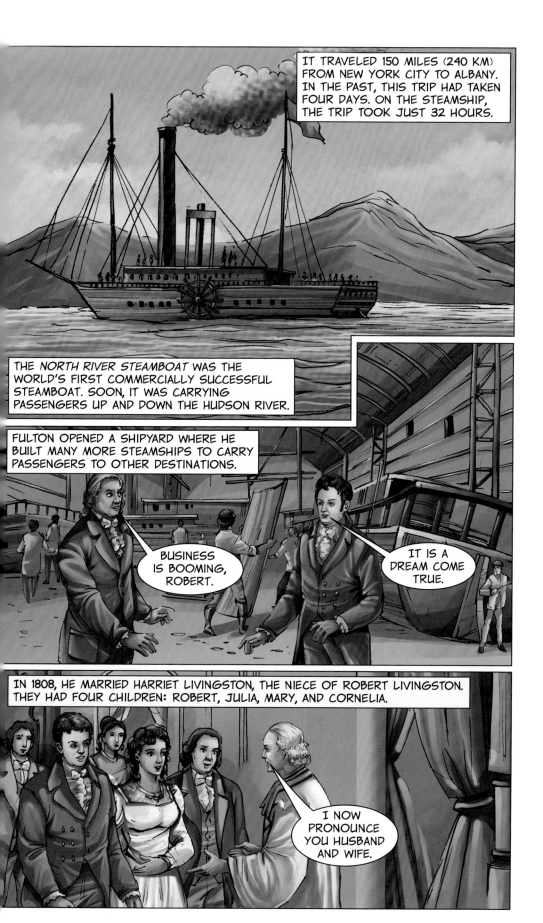

IT TRAVELED 150 MILES (240 KM) FROM NEW YORK CITY TO ALBANY. IN THE PAST, THIS TRIP HAD TAKEN FOUR DAYS. ON THE STEAMSHIP, THE TRIP TOOK JUST 32 HOURS.

THE *NORTH RIVER STEAMBOAT* WAS THE WORLD'S FIRST COMMERCIALLY SUCCESSFUL STEAMBOAT. SOON, IT WAS CARRYING PASSENGERS UP AND DOWN THE HUDSON RIVER.

FULTON OPENED A SHIPYARD WHERE HE BUILT MANY MORE STEAMSHIPS TO CARRY PASSENGERS TO OTHER DESTINATIONS.

BUSINESS IS BOOMING, ROBERT.

IT IS A DREAM COME TRUE.

IN 1808, HE MARRIED HARRIET LIVINGSTON, THE NIECE OF ROBERT LIVINGSTON. THEY HAD FOUR CHILDREN: ROBERT, JULIA, MARY, AND CORNELIA.

I NOW PRONOUNCE YOU HUSBAND AND WIFE.

WHEN THE WAR OF 1812 BROKE OUT, THE US NAVY HIRED FULTON TO BUILD A SHIP TO PROTECT NEW YORK HARBOR FROM THE BRITISH.

THE SHIP FULTON BUILT WAS THE *DEMOLOGOS*, THE WORLD'S FIRST STEAM-POWERED WARSHIP. IT WAS 300 FEET (91 M) LONG, 200 FEET (61 M) WIDE, AND HAD A 120-HORSEPOWER ENGINE. IT MOUNTED 32 GUNS.

ARE YOU OKAY, ROBERT?

IT'S JUST A COLD.

IN HIS HONOR, THE *DEMOLOGOS* WAS RENAMED THE *FULTON*, AND A DAY OF **MOURNING** WAS DECLARED. FULTON LATER RECEIVED A PLACE IN THE HALL OF FAME FOR GREAT AMERICANS.

BEFORE THE *DEMOLOGOS* WAS COMPLETED, FULTON CAUGHT A SEVERE CHEST COLD. HE DIED ON FEBRUARY 24, 1815, AT THE AGE OF 49.

ROBERT FULTON WAS A MAN OF MANY TALENTS. HE WAS AN ARTIST, ENGINEER, AND INVENTOR. HIS SUBMARINE, THE *NAUTILUS*, AND HIS STEAMBOAT, THE *NORTH RIVER STEAMBOAT*, USHERED IN THE **ERA** OF MODERN SEA TRAVEL.

Timeline

1765   Robert Fulton is born on November 14, on a farm in Lancaster County, Pennsylvania.

1782   Fulton moves to Philadelphia at the age of 17 to work as an artist.

1785   Fulton buys a farm in Hopewell, Pennsylvania.

1786   Fulton moves to London, England, to study painting with Benjamin West.

1793   Fulton gives up painting to study civil engineering.

1796   Fulton's *A Treatise on the Improvement of Canal Navigation* is published.

1797   Fulton moves to Paris, France.

1800   Fulton creates the first panorama ever shown in Paris.

          On July 29, Fulton tests the *Nautilus,* the first working submarine.

1801   Fulton meets Robert Livingston, the American ambassador to France, and they decide to build a steamboat together.

1803   Fulton completes the first working model of his steamboat.

1804   Fulton returns to London, England.

1805   In October, Fulton successfully tests the first working torpedo.

1805   On October 21, the British navy defeats the French navy in the Battle of Trafalgar.

1806   Fulton returns to America with a specially-built steam engine.

1807   On August 17, the *North River Steamboat,* also known as the *Clermont,* successfully sails up the Hudson River.

1808   Fulton marries Harriet Livingston, the niece of Robert Livingston.

1814   Fulton completes his design for the *Demologos,* the world's first steam-powered warship.

1815   Robert Fulton dies on February 24 at the age of 49.

Glossary

canals (ka-NALZ) Man-made waterways.

civil engineering (SIH-vul en-juh-NEER-ing) Field of study that involves planning and building engines, machines, roads, and bridges.

commercial (kuh-MER-shul) Having to do with business or trade.

craftsmen (KRAFTS-men) Workmen who practices a certain trade.

detonate (DEH-tun-ayt) To explode or to cause something to explode.

dredging (DREJ-ing) Digging to make a waterway deeper.

era (ER-uh) A period of time or history.

fortunes (FOR-chinz) Riches, health, and good luck.

hull (HUL) The frame, or body, of a ship.

lockets (LO-kets) Small cases that are usually worn on a chain around a person's neck. They often hold a picture of a loved one.

mourning (MORN-ing) Showing or feeling sadness.

nobleman (NOH-bul-man) A man of royalty or of another high-ranking position.

panorama (pa-nuh-RA-muh) A full, wide view of something.

portraits (POR-trezt) A picture, often a painting, of a person.

prominent (PRAH-mih-nent) Well-known, important.

propelled (puh-PELD) To move forward with force.

propeller (puh-PEL-er) Paddlelike parts on an object that spin to move the object forward.

shipped (SHIPD) Sent somewhere for delivery

torpedo (tor-PEE-doh) An underwater missile that blows up when it hits something.

will (WIL) A legal document describing how a person's property will be handled after that person's death.

Index

B

Bonaparte, Napoleon, 10

Boulton and Watt steam
engines, 15, 16

C

*Clermont (North River
Steamboat)*, 18, 19

D

Demologos, 20

F

Franklin, Benjamin, 7

Fulton, Harriet Livingston, 3, 19

Fulton, May Smith, 3, 4

H

Hudson River, 18, 19

L

Livingston, Robert, 3, 13, 14, 15

London, England, 7, 16

N

Nautilus, 10, 11, 12

*North River Steamboat,
(Clermont)* 18, 19

P

Paris, France, 9, 10

Pennsylvania, 4, 6, 7

S

Stanhope, Charles, 3, 8, 9

T

torpedo, 12, 16, 17

W

West, Benjamin, 3, 7, 8

Websites

Due to the changing nature of Internet links, PowerKids Press has developed an online list of websites related to the subject of this book. This site is updated regularly. Please use this link to access the list:

www.powerkidslinks.com/jgai/fult/